I0064515

Help! My Job Sucks

Insider Tips on Making Your Job More Satisfying and Improving Your Career

Business Professional Series #6

Published by The Writing King
www.thewritingking.com

Help! My Job Sucks

Copyright © 2016 by Richard G Lowe, Jr.

All rights reserved. No part of this publication may be reproduced, stored in a retrieval system, or transmitted by any means – electronic, mechanical, photographic (photocopying), recording, or otherwise – without prior permission in writing from the author.

Although every precaution has been taken to verify the accuracy of the information contained herein, the author and publisher assume no responsibility for any errors or omissions. No liability is assumed for damages that may result from the use of information contained within.

Trademarked names appear throughout this book. Rather than use a trademark symbol with every occurrence of a trademarked name, names are used in an editorial fashion, with no intention of infringement of the respective owner's trademark.

Cover Artist: theamateurzone

ASIN: B018IY4INO
ISBN: 978-1-943517-88-6 (Hardcover)
ISBN: 978-1-943517-87-9 (Paperback)
ISBN: 978-1-943517-19-0 (eBook)

Table of Contents

Introduction

"A good job is more than just a paycheck. A good job fosters independence and discipline, and contributes to the health of the community. A good job is a means to provide for the health and welfare of your family, to own a home, and save for retirement." – James H. Douglas, Jr.

Is there such a thing as the perfect job? I'm sure we each have our own definition of perfection in the workplace. Some people prefer to work in the great outdoors, others enjoy the air-conditioned comfort of an office in a skyscraper, and some enjoy working out of an RV.

Regardless, sometimes conditions conspire to make the regular trek to a job feel like a trip through Dante's Inferno. Sometimes, these are out of our control, such as a malicious manager or incompetent colleague.

Years ago, the company where I worked was located in a two-story building, and my department was upstairs. The roof leaked, the carpets were dirty; the walls had bare rafters, and the furniture consisted of hand-me-downs from a dozen different offices.

Nonetheless, it was a great place to work, because the team was a group of brilliant engineers and technicians who were a joy to work with. The projects were challenging, yet achievable, the money paid the bills, and the culture of the company demanded that each employee was a valuable member of the team.

Introduction

On the other hand, I have worked in businesses with absolutely perfect environments, yet were challenging, because the boss was completely whacked. In one case, my supervisor was certified as insane by a psychiatrist, which made it very uncomfortable to work with him as his moods and reactions were completely unpredictable. Needless to say, that job could be a challenge at times.

A characteristic that creates a pleasant work environment is the belief that the company cares, the boss listens, and there is a chance to get ahead and, perhaps, get a raise or promotion. Being taken advantage of often causes the perfect job to become dreary and tedious. Like most of us, I'm sure, bosses have made promises to me in the past to get extra work and longer hours and then reneged when the time came to pay up.

The ideal work environment is free from harassment of all kinds. You should expect to be treated as a human being, although your employer has every right to demand that you put in a solid day's work for a day's pay. Anything that creates a hostile work environment is harassment, but always keep in mind it is the right, in fact, the duty, of an employer to insist that each employee works to their maximum potential.

In fact, one of the characteristics of an excellent job is being supported by your boss and employer, such that you can do the best job possible with the highest quality. The worst places where I have worked had conditions, such that it was impossible to deliver quality service in an competent manner.

Sometimes, one or more team member can intentionally or unintentionally create a workplace environment that is miserable for others. A sarcastic employee, for example, who makes rude and hostile comments can undermine a person's confidence and abilities.

There are times when the knowledge that getting a promotion or raise is not possible makes it onerous to come to work each day. There is no longer an incentive to put in more than the requisite effort, ask for training, and deliver higher-than-expected quality and performance. The goal of getting a paycheck for day-to-day work is often not enough; many of us need that additional incentive, more pay for more responsibility, to make us stretch our efforts.

Another thing to make a job miserable is when you are incompetent at a particular task. The word incompetence is not an insult; it merely means that a person doesn't understand how to do a particular job or task. This can be difficult to fix until it's admitted and understood, and then it's amazing how easy it becomes. Some additional training, perhaps, or even the assignment of a mentor to help out can solve the problem relatively quickly.

Always, the best long-term strategy is to have enough financial depth that you can withstand leaving your job if need be. I recommend you have at least six months' salary in the bank or similarly liquid to enable you to survive long enough to find a new place to work.

Introduction

Check out <u>Help! I've Lost My Job: Tips on What to do When You're Unexpectedly Unemployed</u> for advice on what to do if you decide to leave your job suddenly, or you're pushed out the door.

http://mybooks.space/helplostmyjob

I created this book to provide some simple tips to help you if you find yourself in a situation where you're no longer motivated by your job, or it's become downright detrimental to your health and survival. Throughout my thirty-five year career, I've held positions that were extraordinarily fulfilling, and I've also been in jobs that made me sick, depressed, and totally unmotivated. Unfortunately, recognizing a bad situation is one thing; having the wherewithal, resources, and financial depth to do something about it is another.

I hope you enjoy what I've written and find it to be of some value. If you would like to send me a note about this book, feel free to write me at <u>rich@thewritingking.com</u>. If you enjoyed the book, please write a positive review.

The Work Environment Sucks

"You can't just give someone a creativity injection. You have to create an environment for curiosity and a way to encourage people and get the best out of them." – Ken Robinson

Ideally, the workplace environment should be set up to encourage employees and managers to perform their duties optimally, promptly, and with good quality.

In an office environment, it is the responsibility of the business to provide a comfortable place to work. Temperature controlled air, availability of water, a place to eat lunch, and a place to store food and supplies are not optional.

On top of that, for jobs that require a lot of sitting, comfortable chairs are essential. There's nothing like experiencing back pain, due to sitting in a hard chair day in and day out for months at a time.

A business must also provide an element of safety for its employees. A well-lit parking lot, for example, is important to ensure that employees can get from the office to their cars in the evening. Some measure of security, such as a guard, may also be needed to provide additional safety.

Safety goes further than that, of course, and any dangers in the workplace should be handled when possible. Of course, the assembly line of a factory or the tarmac of an airport may be dangerous, but the business should take all opportunities to make the environment as safe as possible. Also, in environments that are inherently dangerous, safety training is essential.

There are many other things that go into making an environment suitable for work and many other kinds of work environments. Not only that, different people have different definitions for the perfect environment.

I worked in one office that had a leaky roof. My desk, as well as those of my team members, was upstairs, and every time it rained, the water would leak down onto the floor, our desks, and everything else in the room.

This became a real problem when it rained because of the computer equipment on the desks. During the first downpour, I had to make a mad rush to cover all of the machines with tarps to keep them from getting soaked by the water pouring from the ceiling.

To make matters worse, the network was inadequate to support the number of workstations in the office. There were complaints every single day about the speed of the network and how much that impacted productive work.

A difficult work environment is anything that limits your ability to optimally complete the tasks that you need to get your job done. This might be as simple as a lack of supplies, such as paper or pens, or as complex as a leaky roof, lack of air-conditioning, or computer equipment that is painfully slow.

There are times when the environment is dangerous to individuals. For example, someone who has asthma might get sudden attacks as a result of dust in the air ducts, or a building may not have adequate protection from earthquakes, fires, and other disaster situations.

When faced with a non-optimal work environment, you have four choices: live with it, report it, fix it, or move on. I found that most people tend to put up with environments that don't work well for them. For example, the company never did fix the roof that leaked over my office, and computer upgrades are often denied as being "too expensive," which completely ignores the cost of lost productivity.

Living with these kinds of problems results in quite a bit of negativity in the workplace. Because they feel helpless and perhaps abused, people tend to complain about the issues that affect them.

Sometimes, it's better to report a problem to the appropriate person or authorities. Just be sure to create a report that precisely defines the problem and backs up your complaint with facts.

If you found that the building where you're working did not have adequate fire protection, you'd be well within your rights to report it to your manager or personnel. If nothing was done, a report to the local fire department, even anonymously, would be appropriate.

Occasionally, to get a business actually to do something, you have to convince multiple people to make reports. If the computers in the office are so slow that it is affecting your work, it's probably a good bet that others are having the same problem. You might do a quick survey to find out and then ask each of them to make a report. Receiving the same complaint from many different people carries far more weight than those from a single individual.

You have the option of trying to fix it yourself when that's possible. I remember when one person in accounting got fed up with her lunch being stolen every day from the office refrigerator. She bought her own little cube refrigerator and stuck it under a desk. That solved the problem nicely, and she enjoyed her lunch after that without worrying about it being "borrowed" by someone else.

One manager got fed up with her computer being slow. She complained several times and then finally bought herself a new machine, plugged it into the network, and happily worked away on a very fast system.

In another instance, a buyer's computer kept getting infected by viruses. In frustration, she installed her own antivirus application, which solved the problem. The book Safe Computing is Like Safe Sex: You have to practice it to avoid infection goes into detail about things you can do to make your home and work computer safer.

http://mybooks.space/safecomputing

Of course, you see people solving environmental problems all the time. For example, in an office without air-conditioning, workers might bring fans to keep cool. If the parking lot is inadequately lit, workers might escort each other to their cars to feel safer.

Another option is to find a new place of employment. Sometimes, it is easier to move on than it is to deal with problem after problem, especially if they never get corrected. The decision to leave depends, of course, on your financial situation and any other benefits that you might be getting from your employer. Sometimes, a high salary or very satisfying work can compensate for poor working conditions.

It's usually best to try and rectify the situation by reporting it or fixing it yourself, if possible, than it is to leave over an environmental problem. You have to judge each issue you are facing and determine the best approach to take.

For example, I lived in California and thus was very much aware of the possibility of earthquakes. This made it important to me that any building where I worked was adequately reinforced to withstand a relatively large earthquake.

In fact, I've turned down several otherwise excellent job offers due to environmental problems. I turned down one position, a very well paying one, because the location of their office was in a building made of unreinforced brick, which is the worst possible place to be inside during an earthquake. Unreinforced brick buildings tend to crumble very quickly, and the bricks and concrete become deadly missiles flying through the air as the building collapses.

However, out of all of the problems discussed in this book, a poor work environment is probably the easiest to correct or at least confront. Most of these types of issues are relatively minor and tend to be annoyances, rather than something that puts your life in danger. Quite often, a simple report to someone in charge is all that is needed to get the problem corrected. If that fails, you might be able to fix it yourself or at

The Work Environment Sucks

- least come up with a workaround, such as bringing in a fan or your own refrigerator.

A Team Member Sucks

"Teamwork makes the dream work, but a vision becomes a nightmare when the leader has a big dream and a bad team." - John C. Maxwell

We've all worked in places with one or more fellow employees who have made our lives miserable or at least more challenging than necessary.

The gossip is the person who always seems to know the newest rumor, the juiciest dirt on everyone at any time. They ask for your confidence, but you can bet that as soon as you're out of earshot, somebody else knows your secrets. Every workplace seems to have a least one gossip, and they revel in passing along every bit of slime that they can.

Some employees are hostile, occasionally, to the point where they are frightening. I had one team member who always seemed to be angry at everything and everyone, and he would explode at the smallest perceived infractions without warning. It got so bad that the company fired him, and management was so afraid of what he might do that they hired extra security guards for a couple of weeks.

Almost as bad is the employee who is frightened of their own shadow. When talking to them, it's pretty obvious that they have been damaged or hurt in the past, or they're desperately afraid of something. Having a conversation with someone who's always afraid, anxious, or terrified can be quite a challenge, and getting them to do productive work is an even more difficult task.

A Team Member Sucks

In my opinion, the worst fellow team member is the one who is slacking or grossly incompetent at their job. It can be very disheartening to be working hard all day long, doing your best to get the job done with quality and on time, and the person at the desk next to you isn't pulling their weight. Unfortunately, our culture in America tends to discourage the reporting of those who are slacking off, because someone who is not doing their best is letting down all of their team members, as well as the company.

Dealing with these different people can be quite a challenge, especially if they don't work for you or aren't even in your department. For example, the delivery person who comes in twice a day to drop off packages might make disparaging remarks about you in front of others. These comments can be quite devastating, but since the delivery person doesn't even work for your company, it can be difficult to get it to stop.

The book On the Professional Code of Ethics and Business Conduct in the Workplace gives some suggestions on how to handle various problems in the office, including those employees known as "bad apples."

http://mybooks.space/professionalethics

How you handle the situation of the team member who is causing you problems varies, based on the situation, the damage caused, and your situation. Sometimes, all that is needed is a simple conversation, even if only to ask the other person to stay away from you.

Deciding to report a person who is behaving in an unprofessional manner can be difficult. People who report on others are not looked upon lightly in the American workplace. Unless the situation is severe, others may view you as somehow threatening to them.

Making a report can also lead to an investigation, especially if you involve human resources. I have written reports on team members — whether or not they worked for me— to human resources on several occasions, because I don't put up with incompetence or anything else that affects my ability to do my job. In two cases, human resources decided "to be fair" to do an investigation upon me. Of course, I came out smelling like a rose, but it was frustrating nonetheless.

Depending on the size of the company, you may have the option of requesting a transfer to another department, but that may not solve the problem.

And of course, if the situation is unbearable, you can make the choice to leave and go to a different company to work.

The Boss is Whacko

"I put my heart and my soul into my work, and have lost my mind in the process." – Vincent Van Gogh

An unethical, unprofessional, or harassing boss can make life downright unbearable. A good manager understands how to work with people, uses communication well, and is often giving feedback, both good and bad, at regular instances. An excellent leader knows they are part of the team, in addition to being the leader, and acts that way.

Sometimes, the problem is the boss, pure and simple. The Peter Principle is a cause of many incompetent managers. The Peter Principle states that people keep getting promoted until they reach a level where they are not competent and, thus, don't get promoted any further. In other words, they remain stuck where they are incompetent, instead of being demoted back down to their previous position.

An incompetent or uncaring boss can be devastating to a career. One of my managers, in particular, gave a year's notice to his retirement, and during that time, he accomplished nothing of any significance. He didn't want to do anything to rock the boat, since he was so close to leaving, and it was pretty obvious that he wasn't at the top of his game.

The effects of this on the team members and I, as well as my peers, was dramatic. We couldn't get anything approved that wasn't essential for operating the business, and the motivation of the entire department slumped.

The Boss is Whacko

A hostile boss is even worse. If you been working for any length of time, I'm sure you have found yourself in the crosshairs of your manager without really understanding why. It's happened to me on several occasions, and the feeling is quite disconcerting. One day, I was doing well, and the next, I found myself under attack day in and day out.

Micromanagers are always annoying. I tend to be a very responsible person and understand what it takes to get my job done in the most efficient manner. Thus, having my boss hang over my shoulder is not only unappreciated, but it creates unneeded stress and anxiety, thereby being counterproductive.

Sometimes, a supervisor will make promises to get you to do extra work, stay late, or be on call without adequate compensation. Usually, this is in the form of some future — stock or partial ownership perhaps. In my experience, in every case, this has turned out to be vapor, promises made and later withdrawn.

In one case, my boss offered a commission any time any of his employees convinced someone to become a client. When push came to shove, however, the boss reneged, claiming that the effort had been part of a salaried employee's job.

The book Help! My Boss Is Whacko! Tips to Help You Deal with Unprofessional Behavior from Your Boss goes into great detail on what you can do in the situations where your boss is incompetent, unethical, hostile, or insane.

http://mybooks.space/bosswhacko

The best thing you can do in these kinds of situations is to ensure that your financial condition is solid enough where you can move to another company if needed. Sometimes, it's harder said than done, of course, but keeping six months' salary in savings is always a good idea.

Communicating with the boss can help, although it is best to approach the subject gently. A pleasant conversation over lunch can sometimes go a long way towards helping ease this kind of situation.

You Can't Get a Promotion

Sometimes, it seems the only way to get a promotion is to find a new job. Most small companies, at least, don't have clearly written job descriptions, and individuals find themselves doing multiple duties because of a shortage of people. Even in those cases where there is a description of the position, it's often ignored or orally altered dramatically.

Even in the largest companies, the route that one needs to take to get a promotion can be undefined or at the mercy of the opinion of one or two managers. There is virtually never an objective, statistics-based method for determining whether or not a person meets the criteria for promotion.

It would be so much easier if there was a checklist for each position that listed everything that was needed to gain that job title and responsibility. That list could include training, certifications, years of experience, achievements, or any other number of things that need to be done to reach that level.

Unfortunately, I've never seen anything like that. In my experience, promotions come about in one of two ways: either a vacant position needs to be filled, so someone gets promoted, or the manager comes to the opinion that promotion is needed.

In companies with very high turnover, promotions can happen very quickly, since people leave on a regular basis. Unfortunately, high turnover often translates into a hostile environment, poor pay rates, or some other negative factor.

You Can't Get a Promotion

Those businesses that provide very stable, enjoyable workplaces for their employees and give good compensation can reduce turnover significantly. This is especially true for companies that are not growing very quickly. Doing a job in these businesses can be very fulfilling, but promotions can be years or even decades apart.

In my experience, the best way to get a promotion is to begin by defining an understanding of the position that you desire. In other words, get a pen or a computer and write down a list of what is needed for that job.

For example, let's say you were hired to be a receptionist, and you want to get a promotion to the office manager position. You could find out that signing up for classes, reading books, and getting certified will prove you are competent for that position.

This approach has the advantage that even if you don't get promoted, you gain the knowledge and expertise necessary to gain that position. Thus, if you decide to move on to another company, you're already set to move into a higher position than your current one.

You Are Being Harassed

"Intimidation, harassment and violence have no place in a democracy." – Mo Ibrahim

Unfortunately, even in these enlightened days, harassment takes place in the workforce. Quite often, it is much more subtle than in the past, but it exists nonetheless.

Legally, harassment is "unwelcome conduct that is based on race, color, religion, sex (including pregnancy), national origin, age (40 or older), disability, or genetic information. Harassment becomes unlawful where 1) enduring the offensive conduct becomes a condition of continued employment, or 2) the conduct is severe or pervasive enough to create a work environment that a reasonable person would consider intimidating, hostile, or abusive." — The US Equal Employment Opportunity Commission

http://www.eeoc.gov/laws/types/harassment.cfm

To be considered harassment under the law, the environment created by the harassment must be intimidating, hostile, or offensive to reasonable people. Minor offenses are isolated incidents that do not qualify legally as harassment.

Many books and courses deal with the legal aspects of harassment, and most companies have some training in one form or another. If you are being harassed, and it fits into the legal definition of harassment above, then you should work with your human resources department or get legal counsel to resolve the issue.

You Are Being Harassed

Of course, there are forms of harassment that do not fall under the law. A boss who is hostile would create an intimidating environment, for example. You might not be able to handle the situation using the legal system, but it is a harassing environment nonetheless.

In any case, the harassment needs to be dealt with, and you have the option of putting up with it, attempting to correct it, or moving to a new department or company.

In my experience, putting up with harassment is not a viable solution. The attacks, usually verbal, will continue unabated unless stopped. In fact, generally, if no attempt is made to put an end to the harassment, it will just get worse.

Sometimes, harassment begins when a new boss comes on board, replacing the old one, and wants to shake up the department to prove his value. He may think that he has a "honeymoon period" that has to show progress within that time limit. Often, the solution chosen is to encourage, using harassment, some employees to leave by their "own free will."

Harassment that falls under the legal definition should always be pursued using the approved methods within your corporation or brought to the local, state, or federal bodies that govern such things. However, in other instances of hostile work environment, a conversation with the perpetrator can prove helpful.

These conversations can be difficult to confront, especially in the case of one's manager. After all, your manager has a lot of power over you. In fact, "employment at will", meaning an employee can be dismissed for any reason and without warning, is the law in most states in the United States. Thus, it's possible that a conversation can escalate into a firing situation.

Every manager I've ever worked with has welcomed a reasonable conversation about any subject, even those that involve creating a hostile work environment. As long as you keep your wits about you, you should be able to communicate your concerns to your manager, and the two of you might very well be able to come up with a solution to the problem.

The book Help! My Boss Is Whacko! Tips to Help You Deal with Unprofessional Behavior from Your Boss has more information about hostile managers and what to do about them.

http://mybooks.space/bosswhacko

There is also the situation where the harassment is not coming from your manager, but rather from someone else in the organization. This could be a peer, a higher level manager, a consultant, a contractor, or anyone else in the environment.

Being harassed by a higher level manager can be tricky (again, the discussion here is about the non-legal form of harassment), since they have a large amount of power over your future. Harassment by the CFO, COO, CEO or any of the other upper-level managers can create a hostile environment that is difficult to solve. If you find yourself in the crosshairs of one of these managers, your only real option may be to move on to a new company.

You Are Being Harassed

In the case of a peer or non-management employee who is creating a hostile workplace for you, the best option is usually to have a discussion with them and see if you can resolve the situation. Sometimes, the best solution is not to directly address the problem with them, but instead, try to mend fences and improve your relationship with them.

In other words, you might just communicate more with that employee or person who is doing the harassment in a safe and friendly manner. Start talking to them about the weather, the local hiking conditions, or some other relatively safe subject. If you do this, you may find the harassment slowly stops.

You Are Being Taken Advantage of

"There comes a time when you have to stop crossing oceans for people who wouldn't even jump in puddles for you." – Unknown

I know from experience that one of the worst feelings is to realize that you're being taken advantage of by your employer. Salaried employees, those who are paid the same, regardless of the amount of work they put in, are often requested or even required to put in hours far and above acceptable limits.

In the United States, an exempt (salaried) employee should work forty hours per week, and occasionally as much as fifty hours, depending upon the situation. Exempt employees are usually not paid overtime.

If you are a salaried employee, and you're being asked to work more than forty or fifty hours a week without additional compensation, you're being used.

When I was just starting out in the business, it was common for me to work 60 to 80 hour weeks. I felt like my work was valued and willingly put in the extra time without additional income, because I believed in the company and the values and integrity of my manager.

Perhaps, the largest problem with working long hours to get the job done is that your manager or company comes to depend upon that extra time. You might begin by willingly putting in a few eighty hour weeks to get a project done on time, and then discover your manager is creating schedules that depend upon those long weeks to meet the deadlines.

Another area that is frequently abused by companies is the availability of salaried employees after hours. Service-oriented businesses or departments tend to want to improve their service levels by requiring their support employees to carry company phones, so they can be reached at all hours of the day.

Unless you're very careful, you'll find that this becomes unpaid work time very quickly. At first, an occasional support call on a weekend or an evening doesn't appear to be such a big deal. However, by accepting this responsibility and allowing it to grow, you are allowing your company to engage in unethical behavior — and not paying people for work they put in is unethical.

If something requires supported after hours, then personnel need to be hired to perform that support. It is unacceptable for a business to demand this support without compensation. If this is vital to a company's interests, then they should be willing and required to pay for that time. If it's not critical enough to pay an overtime rate for the time, then it shouldn't be done.

For most of my career, I was required to carry a company pager, cell phone, or smart phone all hours of the day. I was never compensated for this time, and I was naïve or stupid enough to accept the requirement. In hindsight, it is an ethical requirement for a business to compensate people just for the mere fact of being on call.

It's usually not a good idea to bring your work home with you. Oh, I know it seems that there's not enough time in the day to get the job done; however, it's better to work towards more efficiency and better prioritization than to pile all your work into your briefcase and continue working while eating dinner at your house.

All that time you spend working after hours at home is unpaid in most situations. You are on your own time, and you will soon find yourself depending on it to meet obligations that you make in the workplace. Worse yet, your manager will assume in his or her schedules that you're putting in that additional time, and you soon find yourself in a trap of your own design. Extricating yourself from that situation can be difficult.

About halfway through my career, I set a firm rule that I didn't bring work home with me. Instead, I ensured that I had my priorities straight and was efficient at doing my job. By understanding priorities, you can work on those things that are important and ignore those things that are not.

If you'd like more information on improving your job, check out the book On the Professional Code of Ethics and Business Conduct in the Workplace.

http://mybooks.space/professionalethics

You Are Incompetent

"There's a lot more to competence than a law degree and a modicum of courtroom skill." – Fred Thompson

Sometimes a person will wind up in a job for which he is not competent. Keep in mind that competence is an acquired trait, and you gain it by becoming educated and experienced. Thus, you can safely say that all of us are incompetent about many things. I'm not a lawyer, so I wouldn't consider myself competent in a courtroom situation.

When you've been promoted to a position, and you haven't received training, nor have any experience, you are going to be making mistakes and not performing as well as you would like. You don't know what you're doing, at least not completely, and that makes you incompetent at that particular job.

This is nothing to be ashamed of, nor should the subject be avoided. It is merely a condition that you need to acknowledge, understand, and correct.

The way to fix incompetence is through focused training, mentoring, and coaching. I've used all three methods, sometimes in combination, and they all work well.

I hired a young man as a systems support technician. As the years went by, his role changed, and new responsibilities were added to his repertoire. He found himself doing database administration, security audits, code reviews, and supporting applications of all types.

You Are Incompetent

He hadn't been trained in these new responsibilities, so quite naturally, he made mistakes, and his performance suffered. He also had this rather annoying habit of trying to cover up his mistakes, which only exacerbated the situation, as it's hard to fix a problem when you don't know it's there.

To correct the situation, I assigned another team member to act as a mentor, and I also sent him to some classes to gain knowledge specific to those areas where he was weak. Finally, I coached him on several situations to help him learn and understand what he needed to do.

When you're managing people, it's always important to look at the performance, skills, and talents of your team members. If you find that they are not doing as well as they should, then you should take steps to correct those areas where they are ignorant and lack experience. Take a look at the book How to be a Good Manager and Supervisor, and How to Delegate for more information about how to manage people.

http://mybooks.space/goodmanager

You don't have to wait for your manager, however. It's usually pretty straightforward to identify areas of your performance that could be improved. You just have to step back and objectively look at your performance, ask yourself a few questions, and come up with some answers.

Do you understand that particular area of your job completely and without reservation? Have you ever been trained to do those tasks? Are you performing as well as you should?

Once you've identified areas that could be improved, you can take steps to make the appropriate corrections.

You could, for example, take a night course or two at the local community college. There are also quite a few websites that give free training for various subjects, and, of course, you can purchase courses on literally anything under the sun.

Sometimes, you can even get your company to pay for courses and schooling. Alternately, if your manager will not approve reimbursement, then you may be able to write off the cost on your taxes. Check with your tax specialist for more information on that.

Being Prepared for Anything

"Victory is the child of preparation and determination." –
Sean Hampton

The most important step you can take is to ensure that you're ready for anything that happens, regarding your job. A job is never guaranteed, and changing or unfortunate circumstances could result in your being laid off or terminated, or you might decide to leave on your own.

It's important to be sure that you maintain adequate money in savings or some other liquid form that you can get to and use if you're unemployed. Of course, unemployment insurance will help — unless you're fired for cause. In that case, you can't collect that form of insurance.

I made it a habit to maintain at least six months of salary in a savings account at all times. This way, if I had to leave my profession, then I had enough cushion to find something else.

Decreasing the amount of debt is also an important way to prepare for anything that happens. Having a large sum of money that you owe to creditors while you're unemployed can be burdensome and very stressful.

Always ensure you are completely up-to-date on your taxes, and you are in good standing with all of the various tax agencies from the local up to the federal level.

Examine your expenses to see if you can cut some luxuries to reduce your debt and maintain money in your savings account. Also, keep in mind that addictions, such as smoking and drinking, are very expensive monetarily, and that money would be better used to build up your cushion in your savings account.

Continuing education is vital. The world is always changing, and these days, the momentum is ever increasing. For you to keep up, you should create a habit of constant improvement.

Take some classes at the local community college on subjects to improve your ability to do your job or to give you the skills needed to do a different job.

If there are certifications available for your profession, then take the prerequisite classes and get certified. Those certificates can be valuable to help provide evidence that you understand a subject to future employers.

Invest in books that will help you in your profession. You can purchase them inexpensively in eBook format or you can buy used volumes through online booksellers at steeply discounted prices.

Constant learning not only will help you in your current job, but it can help you prepare for future jobs as well. The more you learn and understand, the more confident you become.

Prepare for the unexpected. You might believe that your job will last forever, and it might seem that everything is going great, but it won't hurt to understand your options if the worst happens.

The book <u>Help! I've Lost My Job: Tips on What to do When You're Unexpectedly Unemployed</u> contains advice on what to do if you decide to leave your job unexpectedly, or you're pushed out the door. By knowing this information, you can be better prepared if you suddenly need to find a new employer for any reason.

http://mybooks.space/helplostmyjob

Conclusion

I have worked for many companies throughout my career. Each of them was a unique experience, in many ways similar and yet different.

I began my career as a very naïve, trusting young man and gave well beyond the call of duty to help with the startup of a new company. Those were fun times, and I felt needed and was making a contribution to something good.

I willingly put in 80 to 100 hour work weeks, without additional compensation, on a regular basis for several years, until I literally burned myself out and had to reduce back to a "normal" work week. This caused much consternation with my manager, who had come to expect the much higher level of productivity that I'd been generating.

As I moved forward through my career, I learned that it was unwise to put in so many hours, regardless of compensation. It's not good for one's health to be so focused that everything else in life disappears. Working those long hours makes it difficult to support a family, continue one's education, and have a life outside of work.

My managers have been all over the spectrum in their competence and mental stability. Some of them have been grossly incompetent, one of them was certified insane, and all of them were human and made the standard mistakes you would expect from time to time.

Conclusion

The main lesson that I learned is to take control of my life and not let others control me beyond the boundaries of the workplace.

When you agree to work for a company, you agree to certain rules, regulations, and procedures. Boundaries exist, sometimes they are documented, and sometimes are assumed without ever being verbalized.

The company also agrees to follow the rules and to have certain obligations. This includes receiving fair compensation for your work, providing a good workplace, ensuring that you can continue to educate yourself to become better at your profession, and to provide competent management.

One of your jobs, as an employee, is to make sure that all of the obligations and responsibilities are fulfilled on both sides of the fence. In other words, ensure that you do your job as agreed and be sure that your company fulfills its responsibilities as agreed.

You must always be on your guard to prevent work from encroaching on other areas of your life. Believe me, unless well-controlled, work can become a monster that engulfs your entire life.

On the other hand, under the right circumstances, a job can be one of the most fulfilling and wonderful experiences of your life. Nothing beats the feeling of being able to contribute and deliver a product or service successfully, with high quality, and on time.

And there is nothing better than being part of a team that is supportive, understanding, and well-managed.

Before you go

If you scroll to the last page in this eBook, you will have the opportunity to leave feedback and share the book with Before You Go. I'd be grateful if you turned to the last page and shared the book.

Also, if you have time, please leave a review. Positive reviews are incredibly useful. If you didn't like the book, please email me at rich@thewritingking.com and I'd be happy to get your input.

linkedin.thewritingking.com

About the Author

https://www.linkedin.com/in/richardlowejr
Feel free to send a connection request

Follow me on Twitter: @richardlowejr

Richard Lowe has leveraged more than 35 years of experience as a Senior Computer Manager and Designer at four companies into that of a bestselling author, blogger, ghostwriter, and public speaker. He has written hundreds of articles for blogs and ghostwritten more than a dozen books and has published manuscripts about computers, the Internet, surviving disasters, management, and human rights. He is currently working on a ten-volume science fiction series – the Peacekeeper Series – to be published at the rate of three volumes per year, beginning in 2016.

Richard started in the field of Information Technology, first as the Vice President of Consulting at Software Techniques, Inc. Because he craved action, after six years he moved on to work for two companies at the same time: he was the Vice President of Consulting at Beck Computer Systems and the Senior Designer at BIF Accutel. In January 1994, Richard found a home at Trader Joe's as the Director of Technical Services and Computer Operations. He remained with that incredible company for almost 20 years before taking an early retirement to begin a new life as a professional writer. He is currently the CEO of The Writing King, a company that provides all forms of writing services, the owner of The EBay King, and a Senior Branding Expert for LinkedIn Makeover. You can find a current list of all books on his Author Page and

About the Author

take a look at his exclusive line of coloring books at The Coloring King.

Richard has a quirky sense of humor and has found that life is full of joy and wonder. As he puts it, "This little ball of rock, mud, and water we call Earth is an incredible place, with many secrets to discover. Beings fill our corner of the universe, and some are happy, and others are sad, but each has their unique story to toll."

His philosophy is to take life with a light heart, and he approaches each day as a new source of happiness. Evil is ignored, discarded, or defeated; good is helped, enriched, and fulfilled. One of his primary interests is to educate people about their human rights and assist them to learn how to be happy in life.

Richard spent many happy days hiking in national parks, crawling over boulders, and peering at Indian pictographs. He toured the Channel Islands off Santa Barbara and stared in fascination at wasps building their homes in Anza-Borrego. One of his joys is photography, and he has photographed more than 1,200 belly dancing events, as well as dozens of Renaissance fairs all over the country.

Because writing is his passion, Richard remains incredibly creative and prolific; each day he writes between 5,000 and 10,000 words, diligently using language to bring life to the world so that others may learn and be entertained.

Richard is the CEO of The Writing King, which specializes in fulfilling any writing need. You can find out more at https://www.thewritingking.com/, and emails are welcome at rich@thewritingking.com

Books by Richard G Lowe Jr.

Business Professional Series

On the Professional Code of Ethics and Business Conduct in the Workplace – Professional Ethics: 100 Tips to Improve Your Professional Life - have you ever wondered what it takes to be successful in the professional world? This book gives you some tips that will improve your job and your career.

Help! My Boss is Whacko! - How to Deal with a Hostile Work Environment - sometimes the problem is the boss. There are all kinds of managers, some competent, some incompetent, and others just plain whacked. This book will help you understand and handle those different types of managers.

Help! I've Lost My Job: Tips on What to do When You're Unexpectedly Unemployed – suddenly having to leave your job can be a harsh and emotional time in your life. Learn some of the things that you need to consider and handle if this happens to you.

Help! My Job Sucks Insider Tips on Making Your Job More Satisfying and Improving Your Career – sometimes conditions conspire to make the regular trek to a job feel like a trip through Dante's Inferno. Sometimes, these are out of our control, such as a malicious manager or incompetent colleague. On the other hand, we can take control of our lives and workplace and improve our situation. Get this book to learn what you can do when your job sucks.

Books by Richard G Lowe Jr.

How to Manage a Consulting Project: Make money, get your project done on time, and get referred again and again – I found that being a consultant is a great way to earn a living. Managing a consulting project can be a challenge. This book contains some tips to help you so you can deliver a better product or service to your customers.

How to be a Good Manager and Supervisor, and How to Delegate – Lessons Learned from the Trenches: Insider Secrets for Managers and Supervisors – I've been a manager for over thirty years I learned many things about how to get the job done and deliver quality service. The information in this book will help you manage your projects to a high level of quality.

Focus on LinkedIn – Learn how to create a LinkedIn profile and to network effectively using the #1 business social media site.

Home Computer Security Series

Safe Computing is Like Safe Sex: You have to practice it to avoid infection – Security expert and Computer Executive, Richard Lowe, presents the simple steps you can take to protect your computer, photos and information from evil doers and viruses. Using easy-to-understand examples and simple explanations, Lowe explains why hackers want your system, what they do with your information, and what you can do to keep them at bay. Lowe answers the question: how to you keep yourself say in the wild west of the internet.

Books by Richard G Lowe Jr.

<u>Disaster Preparation and Survival Series</u>

<u>Real World Survival Tips and Survival Guide: Preparing for and Surviving Disasters with Survival Skills</u> – CERT (Civilian Emergency Response Team) trained and Disaster Recovery Specialist, Richard Lowe, lays out how to make you, your family, and your friends ready for any disaster, large or small. Based upon specialized training, interviews with experts and personal experience, Lowe answers the big question: what is the secret to improving the odds of survival even after a big disaster?

<u>Creating a Bug Out Bag to Save Your Life: What you need to pack for emergency evacuations</u> - When you are ordered to evacuate—or leave of your free will—you probably won't have a lot of time to gather your belongings and the things you'll need. You may have just a few minutes to get out of your home. The best preparation for evacuation is to create what is called a bug out bag. These are also known as go-bags, as in, "grab it and go!"

<u>Professional Freelance Writer Series</u>

<u>How to Operate a Freelance Writing Business, and How to be a Ghostwriter – Proven Tips and Tricks Every Author Needs to Know about Freelance Writing: Insider Secrets from a Professional Ghostwriter</u> – This book explains how to be a ghostwriter, and gives tips on everything from finding customers to creating a statement of work to delivering your final product.

<u>How to Write a Blog That Sells and How to Make Money From Blogging: Insider Secrets from a Professional Blogger:</u>

Books by Richard G Lowe Jr.

<u>Proven Tips and Tricks Every Blogger Needs to Know to Make Money</u> – There is an art to writing an article that prompts the reader to make a decision to do something. That's the narrow focus of this book. You will learn how to create an article that gets a reader interested, entices them, informs them, and causes them to make a decision when they reach the end.

Other Books by Richard Lowe Jr

How to Be Friends with Women: How to Surround Yourself with Beautiful Women without Being Sleazy – I am a photographer and frequently find myself surrounded by some of the most beautiful women in the world. This book explains how men can attract women and keep them as friends, which can often lead to real, fulfilling relationships.

How to Throw Parties like a Professional: Tips to Help You Succeed with Putting on a Party Event – Many of us have put on parties, and I know it can be a daunting and confusing experience. In this book, I share what I learned from hosting small house parties to shows and events.

Additional Resources

Is your career important to you? Find out how to move your career in any direction you desire, improve your long-term livelihood, and be prepared for any eventuality. Visit the page below to sign up to receive valuable tips via email, and to get a free eBook about how to optimize your LinkedIn profile.

http://list.thewritingking.com/

I've written and published many books on a variety of subjects. They are all listed on the following page.

https://www.thewritingking.com/books/

On that site, I also publish articles about business, writing, and other subjects. You can visit by clicking the following link:

https://www.thewritingking.com

To find out more about me or my photography, you can visit these sites:

Personal website: https://www.richardlowe.com
Photography: http://www.richardlowejr.com
LinkedIn Profile: https://www.linkedin.com/in/richardlowejr
Twitter: https://twitter.com/richardlowejr

If you have any comments about this book, feel free to email me at rich@thewritingking.com

Premium Writing Services

Do you have a story that needs to be told? Have you been trying to write a book for ages but never can seem to find the time to get it done? Do you want to brand your business, but don't know how to get started?

The Writing King has the answer. We can help you with any of your writing needs.

Ghostwriting. We can write your book, which entails interviewing you to get your story, writing the book and then working with you to revise it until complete. To discuss your book, contact The Writing King today.

Website Copy. Many businesses include the text on their sites as an afterthought, and that can result in lost sales and leads. Hire The Writing King to review your site and recommend changes to the text which will help communicate your message and improve your sales.

Blogging. Build engagement with your customers by hiring us to write a weekly or semi-weekly article for your blog, LinkedIn or other social media. Contact The Writing King today to discuss your blogging needs.

LinkedIn. LinkedIn is of the most important vehicles for finding new business, and a professionally written profile works to pulling in those leads. Write or update your profile today.

Technical Writing. We have broad experience in the computer, warehousing and retail industries, and have

Premium Writing Services

written hundreds of technical documents. Contact The Writing King today to find out how we can help you with your technical writing project.

The Writing King has the skills and knowledge to help you with any of your writing needs. Call us today to discuss how we can help you.